Jokes to help you l

A joke is un chiste, and it is good to have a laugh, or even just a smile. Rather than writing una lista de chistes, I have written some micro Spanish lessons, and used los chistes to use the Spanish in context. I tried to start with the laugh and work backwards, so it isn't your typical Spanish course, but I found that I could explain some really useful Spanish around some of my favourite jokes.

I haven't written los chistes completamente in Spanish. I have just used them to illustrate a few words. I have kept the explanations to the little Spanish lessons, and mostly kept explanations out of the jokes themselves. I felt it was best that way.

I don't stick to English or Spanish. From my point of view, until you can understand enough to learn Spanish in Spanish, the mixing is essential. Lots of Spanish teachers prefer pure Spanish, but then they already speak Spanish. I just don't want you to have to work that hard!

¡Por favor, enjoy los chistes!

Ruth Darby, April 2020

Contents

Jokes to help you learn Spanish

Ruth Darby

SPANGLISH FANTASTICO

Pronunciation

"e" gets a sound every time, even at the end of a word.

"ge" sounds like /hey/. Inteligente is said, /in-telly-hen-tay/.

"gi" sounds like /hee/. Gimnasio is said, /heem-na-seeo/.

"u" normally makes an /oo/ sound, never a /yoo/ sound.

"j" always makes a /h/ sound.

"h" is silent. Hola is said /ola/.

"qu" makes a /k/ sound, like in mosquito.

"ll" makes a /y/ sound, like in Marbella, /mar-be-ya/.

"ñ" makes a /ny/ sound, like ny in the word canyon.

Punctuation

Questions have a question mark at the beginning and at the end, like brackets or speech marks do in English. Exclamation marks are the same, one at either side.

Bill Santiago on Spanglish 101, available on YouTube, points out how much more excited the Spanish language is. The exclamation mark at the beginning of the exclamation tells readers to get ready to be excited before they even know why. It's worth a watch.

Guidance is given throughout the text.

Jokes to help you learn Spanish

HOW TO LAUGH, JA JA JA

Hola. Mi nombre es Ruth. **A joke**, in Spanish, is **un chiste**. Before we make a start, you had better know how to laugh in Spanish. The letter H is mute, so if you laughed like this:

— Ha ha ha

It would sound like **un chimpancé**, that is **a chimpanzee**: "a a a". Or like **a seal**, that's **una foca**: "a a a". As you don't want to sound like una foca, you need to laugh like this:

— Ja ja ja

It's the same sound we make when we laugh in English, it's just written differently because, en español, the letter j makes the /h/ sound.

So when your amigos text you un chiste, don't text back ha ha ha. Text back ja ja ja. And if your amigos ask why, tell them:

— I'm learning español, and I don't want to sound like una foca.

The word **relajar** means **to relax**, so that's not difícil. I like it when words are not difíciles. **English** is **inglés**. No es difícil. **Spanish** is **español**. No es difícil. If I talk about both of them at the same time, I have to make the word difícil plural: difíciles.

No es means **it isn't**. **No son** means **they aren't**. **Y** means **and**, pronounced /ee/. Inglés y español no son difíciles. Can you understand that?

What is the word for relax? Relajar.

— Why is it nice to learn Spanish by talking about jokes, about chistes?
— Because it's good to relaja ja jar.

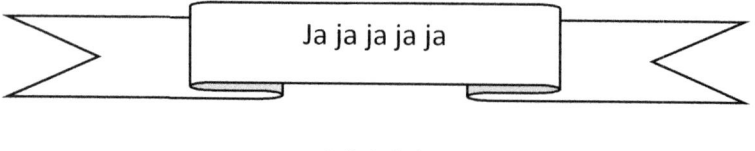

Ja ja ja ja ja

* * * * *

FUNNY ORANGE

Diversión means **fun**. If you print off a "Diversion ends" traffic sign, and stick it on the exit door to the languages corridor in your school, your profesor de español might like that. As you leave la zona de lenguajes, diversión ends. I'm telling you this because it might help you to remember the next word, which is divertido. **Divertido** means **funny**, and it's a word we are going to need as we are talking about chistes, to help you learn español. You might think all of the chistes I talk about are divertidos. You might not.

You might notice that, just like the word difícil, divertido also becomes plural when it is about more than one thing. En español things are masculine or feminine. When something **masculine** is funny, **es divertido**. When something **feminine** is funny, **es divertida**.

The word for **orange** en español is una **naranja**. En inglés our word for orange used to be norange, apparently. Norange became orange because a norange sounds like an orange. I think that **is funny, es divertido**. I also think that norange is closer to the word en español, naranja. Naranja es un color y naranja es una fruta, just like en inglés. The word for **which** is **cuál**. See if you can understand the next chiste.

— ¿Cuál fruta es la fruta más divertida en español?

— Una naranja ja ja.

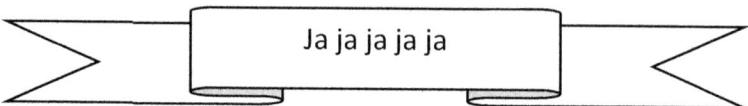

Ja ja ja ja ja

Use the Spanish

Give your opinion.

- No es difícil = It's not difficult.

- Es divertido = It's fun/ It's funny.

Ask for an orange.

- Una naranja, por favor = An orange, please.

---

* * * * *

SPANISH FIREMEN

En mi opinión, chistes can really help you with your pronunciación when you are learning español.

The letter J makes a /h/ sound, so the Spanish equivalente of the name Joseph is José, and it sounds like /Hose A/. You might know how to ask someone's name en español:

¿Cómo te llamas? The double LL makes a /y/ sound, so llamas sounds like /yamas/. To ask, **what do you call**, the Spanish is very similar: **¿Cómo se llama?** If you are asking about more than one thing or more than one persona, it becomes ¿cómo se llaman? **¿Cómo se llaman?** means **what are they called**.

The number **two** is **dos**. The word for **firemen** is quite a nice word, it is **bomberos**. I like the way that sounds: bomberos. To help you remember, just think that firemen would, probablemente, be parte of any team sent to deal with a bomb, so they are bomberos. The word for **next** is **próximo**. Now see if you can understand el próximo chiste.

— ¿Cómo se llaman los dos bomberos españoles?
— Hose-A and Hose-B.

The word for **fire** is **fuego**, so the word "bomberos" is nothing like a literal translation of **firemen**, which would be **fuego-hombres**, or something like that.

— If you are tempted to fight fuego with fuego, remember que los bomberos usually use agua.

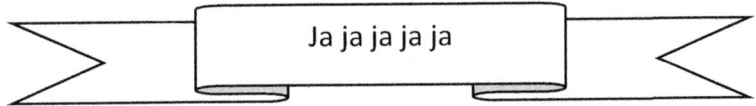

Ja ja ja ja ja

THE QU SOUND IS /K/

The letters qu make a /k/ sound in Spanish. It's easy to remember if you think of the Spanish word we have borrowed, mosquito. They have knock knock chistes en español. Instead of saying **knock knock**, you can say **toc toc**. To say who is there, they say who is it. **Who is it**, en español, is **¿quién es?** Of course, quién starts with a /k/ sound, because en español the letters qu make a /k/ sound. Have a read of this one:

— Toc toc.

— ¿Quién es?

— Amos.

— ¿Amos quién?

— No, Amos Quito.

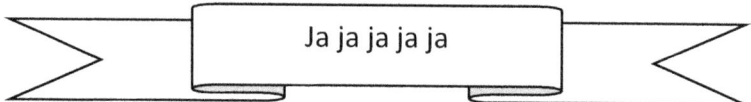

Ja ja ja ja ja

I love some of the words with the /k/ sound. Uno de mis favoritos is maquillaje. La pronunciación es /makky-yahey/, y en mi opinión that sounds great. What does **maquillaje** mean? It is **makeup**, as in mascara, blusher and lipstick. Do you like that word? Try saying it: maquillaje. I also like that mascara sounds a bit like mask and cara. **Cara** is **face** in Spanish, so when you wear máscara as it's known in Latin America, or rímel as it's known en España, you are masking your cara a little bit. Los chistes about maquillaje tend to be unkind, and I don't think unkind is divertido.

Another word that I like is equivalente, which sounds like /ekee-valentay/. El equivalente español de John is Juan. La pronunciación es /hwan/. It sounds great. En mi opinión it sounds great.

— How many Spanish men does it take to change a light bulb?

— Just Juan.

Use the Spanish

Meet someone at your door.

- ¿Quién es? = Who is it?
- ¿Cómo te llamas? = What are you called?

---

* * * * *

GUESS = ADIVINAR

I like the word adivinar. If you don't know a word it is great if you can just adivina and move on. Adivinar es un tipo de inteligencia. The word for **very** is **muy**: /mweeeee/. If you are happy to adivinar, you are muy inteligente, en mi opinión.

I like the word adivinar because it sounds a bit like "ah divven na," which means I don't know, en el acento regional de los Geordies in the north-east of Inglaterra.

Casa is **house**. **Mi casa es tu casa** means **make yourself at home**. **A retirement home** is **una casa de ancianos**. Mi mamá never wants to live en una casa de ancianos. I think she just doesn't want to think of herself as una anciana, and who can blame her!

— En el futuro, en la casa de ancianos, los residentes can play games of "adivina qué mi tatuaje used to be."

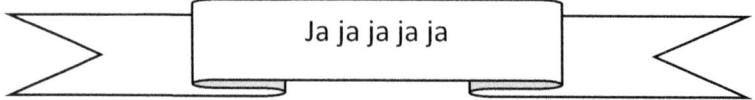

Ja ja ja ja ja

Can you adivinar what tatuaje means? /Ta-too-a-hey/. I bet you can. Eres muy inteligente. You are goint to need that inteligencia, and that ability to adivinar, to read this book!

> **Use the Spanish**
>
> Describe yourself or a friend
>
> - (Eres) muy inteligente = (You are) very intelligent
>
> Make a guest welcome
>
> - Mi casa es tu casa = My house is your house

TIME IN SPANISH

Time is easy en español. **Hora**, the word for **hour**, is often used to talk about time. To eat is comer, and **dinner time** is **hora de comer**. Comestibles are things you eat. Comer is to eat. You can remember that! **Tiempo** also means **time**. **Tiempo libre** is **free time**. No es difícil. But the word for clock es diferente, mucho más diferente. The word for **clock** is **reloj**. The letter J makes a /h/ sound, which is a bit strange for the end of a word. Try saying it: reloj. **A loss** is **una perdida**. En inglés, perdition means the loss of everything or even the loss of your soul! This makes it easier for us English speakers to remember that perdida means loss.

— Have you ever tried to comer un reloj?

— Es un perdida de tiempo!

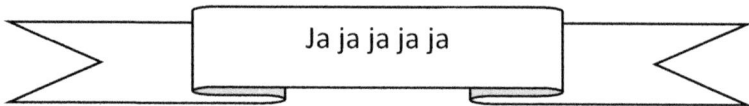

Ja ja ja ja ja

To ask, **what time is it**, you say, **¿qué hora es?** It sounds like this: /kay ora es/. To answer, you just need **los números, the numbers**, so let's run through them now.

01.00 = la una. 02.00 = las dos. 03.00 = las tres. 04.00 = las cuatro. 05.00 = las cinco. 06.00 = las seis. 07.00 = las siete. 08.00 = las ocho. 09.00 = las nueve. 10.00 = las diez. 11.00 = las once /las on-say/. 12.00 = las doce /las do-say/.

So you can ask, ¿qué hora es? You can answer, las once, or whatever hour it is. Right now, for me, **son las diez y media, it's half past ten.**

To ask, **what is the matter**, say, **¿qué pasa?** That is quite a nice thing to say. Try it now: ¿qué pasa? It is also like saying, what's up? ¿Qué pasa? Let's try otro chiste.

— I met un loco en la avenida, a crazy man in the avenue.

— He asked me, - Perdone, ¿Qué hora es?

— I looked at mi reloj. - Son las cuatro y media.

— El loco looked miserable and threw his hands en el aire. Concerned, I asked, - ¿Qué pasa?

— Nada, it's just that every time I ask, I get a different answer.

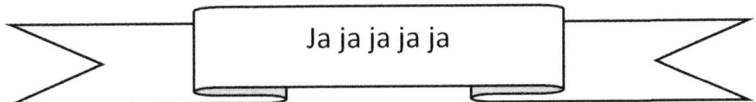

Ja ja ja ja ja

Nada is a great word. It means **nothing**. One of my favourite things to say en español is **absolutely nothing**. It sounds like this: **ab-so-lu-ta-men-tay nada**. You can get such emphasis with las seis sílabas in the word absolutamente.

Nada is a word that has two meanings en español. **Nadar** is **to swim**, and **he swims**, or **he is swimming**, is **nada**. You already know, nada also means nothing.

The word for **fish** is **pez**. **Ese** means **that**, so how do you say "that fish"? Ese pez. Did you get it right? **Mis estudiantes** means **my students**. I tell mis estudiantes to think of pisces, the astrological signo which is a fish. Do that, and you can conectar the Spanish word pez with the English words, pisces and fish. **Hace** means **he does**, or **he is doing**. It sounds like /a-say/. The word for **what** is **¿qué?** It sounds like this: /kay/. Ready for un chiste?

— ¿Qué hace ese pez?

— Nada.

Do you understand? Nada means nothing and he swims!

Use the Spanish

Find out what time it is

- ¿Qué hora es? = What time is it?

- Es hora de comer = It's dinner time

Find out what people are up to

- ¿Qué pasa? = What's happening?

- ¿Qué hace? = What's he/ she doing?

- Absolutamente nada = Absolutely nothing

---

* * * * *

SPANISH WINE

Another Spanish word with two meanings is vino. **Vino** means **wine**. Of course, wine and whine sound the same.

— What is a Spanish teacher's favourite wine?

— "I want to go to Marbella!"

The letter v often makes a /b/ sound en español, so vino sounds a bit like the Beano. Does your mamá like a cheeky copa de vino?

The other meaning of the word **vino** is **he came**, **she came** or **it came**. Normalmente, you can tell who you are talking about, so you don't need the words for **he** and **she**, **él** and **ella**, but if you want emphasis or clarity, you can say él vino or ella vino.

There are four basic tastes in the human palette: salty, sweet, acidic and bitter. En español, that is, **salada** for **salty**, **dulce** for **sweet**, ácida, and **bitter** is **amarga**. (If a type of food is masculine, it could be ácido or amargo for acidic or bitter). Amarga can also describe una persona, por ejemplo your mother in law could be amarga, or you could be amarga. If you are a man, you could be amargo.

I like the word for **mother in law** en español: **suegra**. It sounds like this: /swegra/. Isn't that nice? If you have a mother in law you can use this new word to greet her: hola suegra. Guess what father in law is! Did you guess suegro? Then you are correcto.

¿Cuál? That is the word for **which**. See if you can understand el próximo chiste:

— ¿Cuál es el vino más amargo de España?

— Vino mi suegra.

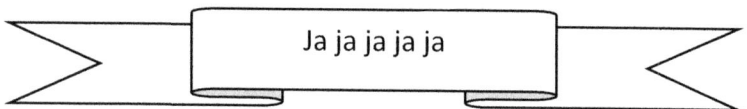

Ja ja ja ja ja

Y el próximo chiste, no es un chiste, precisamente. It is more like a tongue twister, or just a play on words. The word for **vinegar** is **vinagre**. Imagina que un vino was very, very ácido, it might taste like vinagre. Remember that vino means wine and it came. The word for **when** is **cuando**. Look up the song Quando Quando Quando. That is how they say **when** en italiano, and only the spelling es diferente en español. The words go like this:

— Tell me when will you be mine!

— Tell me cuando cuando cuando!

I used the Spanish spelling.

Right, in Spanish, how would you say, when the wine came, it wasn't wine that came, it was vinegar that came. How would you say that? You would say it like this:

— Cuando vino el vino

— No vino vino

— Vino vinagre.

If you are en un restaurante, it is likely that you will have a waiter. A **waiter** is un **camarero**. Imagina que el camarero se llama Cameron, and he comes from Cameroon. **De dónde** means **from where**. Dónde is a nice word, like a day belonging to Don. Where could that happen? ¿Dónde?

Vino means **he came** or **she came**. **Vengo** means **I come**. **Venir** means **to come**. **De la casa** means **from the house**. So **vino de la casa** means **he came from the house**. It also means house wine.

— El camarero en un restaurante says, - ¿Vino de la casa, señor?

— El cliente responde, - What is it to you, de dónde vengo?!

* * * * *

POCO Y MUCHO, HUSBANDS AND WIVES

Un poco means **a little** or **a bit**. **Un poco de español** is **a little bit of Spanish**. **Un poco de vino** is **a little bit of wine**. I like un poco de magia. Gi makes a /hee/ sound, so la pronuncicación is /ma-heea/. Do you like un poco de magia? **A magician** is **un mago**. G only makes that /h/ sound when the next letter is e or i. So la pronunciación of mago is /ma-go/. **There was** is **había**.

— Había un mago méxicano. He said, "uno, dos …" then he disappeared without a tres.

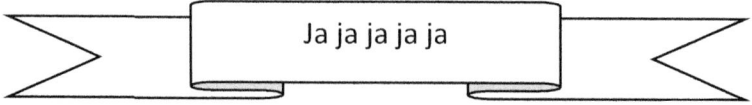

Ja ja ja ja ja

Un poco de means **a little** or **a bit**. **Un poco de diversión** means **a little bit of fun**. **Mucho diversión** means **a lot of fun**. **Un hombre** is **a man**, and **una viuda** is **a widow**. **Su marido** is **her husband**. I quite like that **marido** is **husband**. You married your marido, right?

— Un hombre walks up to una viuda at the funeral de su marido.

— Can I say just one word? – he asks.

— Sí, claro, – la viuda responde.

— Mucho, - says el hombre.

— Gracias, - says la viuda. – That means a lot.

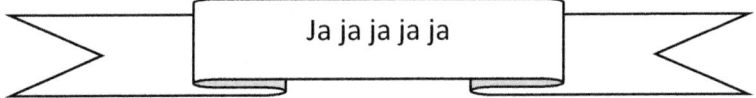

Ja ja ja ja ja

Un marido is **a husband**. It is such a nice word It seems unfair, injusto that the word for wife is not nearly so nice. **Wife** is **mujer**, pronounced /moo-hair/. You might think it is **more fair**, **más justo**, that there are other words for **husband and wife: esposo y esposa**. Then you find out that **esposas** also means **handcuffs**, and it seems injusto once again.

— Mi esposa used to hit me with stringed instrumentos.

— She had una historia de violíncia.

A drummer is **un baterista**, or **una baterista** if it is a female drummer. El baterista en la banda se llama Rufus Taylor. Es un ejemplo. **Ella** is **she**, like the girl's name, but you say /eya/ because double LL makes a /y/ sound en español. Just think of tortillas, Marbella, Mallorca and paella.

— I wrote a song about tortillas.

— Actually, it's more of a rap.

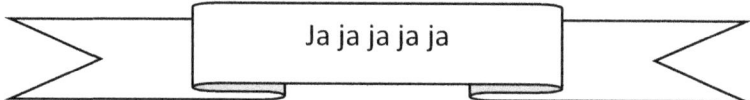

Ja ja ja ja ja

You should say the LL in all Spanish words as a /y/ sound. **Él** means **he**. **Preguntó** is **he asked** or **she asked**. If you want to make it absolutamente claro, you can say, él preguntó or ella preguntó. **Answered** is **respondió**. Again, if you want más claridad, you can say él respondió or ella respondió.

Here is un chiste about un baterista.

— La mujer de un baterista had quadruplets. He wanted to nombrar each one of them Anna.

— Ella preguntó, how will we tell them apart?

— Él respondió, Anna uno, Anna dos, Anna tres, Anna cuatro!

* * * * *

CON, SIN Y FAMILIA

You can say "again" a few different ways en español. **Otra vez** is literally **another time**, but basicamente, it means **again**. **De nuevo** means **again** too. **Nuevo** means **new**, on

24

its own. Let's talk about la hora otra vez. **La hora** means **time**. The letter H makes no sound, so "hora" sounds exactamente igual a "**ora**", which means **pray**. En inglés oration means a formal public speech, but it is not a word in common use.

Con means **with**. Think of context, or chili con carne, which means chili with meat. No good for me, I'm vegetariana. Another word that has conexiones con la religión is **pecados**, which means **sins**. There was a very nice fish restaurante en Lima, Perú, when I lived there, called *Los Siete Pecados.* **Un pez** is **a fish** when it is alive, but **fish ready to eat** is called **pescado**, so los siete pecados was a play on pecado = sin, and pescado = fish. I was quite proud of the translation I gave it: The Seven Deadly Fins. Maybe shouldn't have put the word "Deadly" in there for un restaurante, though.

Padre means **father**, and it is used, even in English, to refer to priests. It isn't just padre that is used for people who aren't actually in your familia. Sometimes, in English, people call boys, my son, even when there is no relation. It also happens en español, where the word for **son** is **hijo**. La pronunciación of hijo is /ee-ho/. **My son is mi hijo.**

— ¿Padre, what can I do for mis pecados?

— Ora, mi hijo. Ora.

— Las once y media padre.

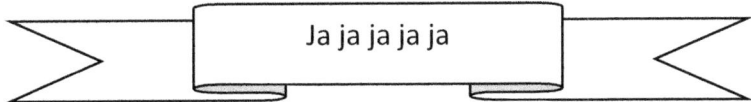

Ja ja ja ja ja

Un niño is **a child**, where **un hijo** is **a son**. Es una diferencia subtil. Just remember, the letter Ñ makes a /ny/ sound, so niño is /neen-yo/. That Ñ also means that the English word **canyon**, and the Spanish translation, **cañon**, sound pretty similar. You know that **a father** is **un padre**. **A mother** is **una madre**. **Una señora** is **a lady**.

Cinco años is **five years**. **Cinco anos** is **five anuses**, so that letter Ñ can make quite a diferencia. En español you don't give your age by saying, I am five years old, you say, **I have five years**. **Tengo cinco años**, not tengo cinco anos.

This next chiste is actually a mini story by the Nobel Prize winning autor colombiano, Gabriel Garcia Márquez. It's about un niño at **una feria, a fair**.

— Un niño de cinco años, who had lost his madre in the crowd de una feria, went up to un agente de la policía and asked him,

— Have you seen una señora walking, without un niño como yo?

— Fin.

Tu hijo is **your son**. The word sounds a bit like a donkey braying: /ee-ho/. **Tu hija** is **your daughter**. That sounds like this: /ee-ha/. They are quite strange sounding words.

Call is **llamar**, and you might know that from questions like ¿cómo te llamas? You might know that **I am called Bob** is **yo me llamo Bob**. Llamar is not just about names, it is also call as in shout to or telephone. Tu madre can say, - Llama a Betty to help you set the table, (if your sister se llama Betty).

Un jefe is **a boss**, and because the letter J makes a /h/ sound, say /hefay/. **Llamar** is **to call**, and **ha llamado** is **has called**. As I say, it could be called on el teléfono. **Algún** means **any**, or some. **Usted** is the respectful or formal word for **you**. **Primero** means **first**.

— Un jefe a su secretaria: - ¿ha llamado algún estúpido?

— No jefe. Usted es el primero.

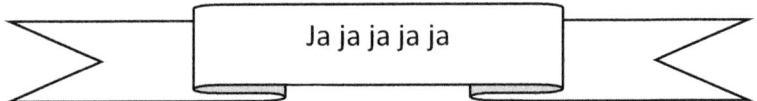

Ja ja ja ja ja

Continuing with the word **llamar**, **to call**, and for este chiste you need the word for **cowboy: un vaquero**. Remember, v often makes a /b/ sound en español, and qu always make a /k/ sound, so vaquero is /ba-ke-ro/. You might also like to know, as cowboys often wore jeans, the word for **jeans** in Spanish is also **vaqueros**.

— ¿Cómo llama el vaquero a su hija?

— ¡Hi-jaaaaaaaaaaaaaaa!

Use the Spanish

Introduce people

- Mi hijo = My son
- Mi hija = My daughter
- Mi jefe = My boss
- Un agente de la policia = A police officer

---

* * * * *

COMO = I EAT, LIKE AND HOW

Pero means **but**. **Pera** means **pear**, as in la fruta. **Tengo** means **I have**. I could say, tengo una pera, pero no tengo una naranja ja ja. Do you remember what **naranja** means? It is an **orange**. A norange.

The word for **apple** is una **manzana**. **Sana** means **healthy**, and manzana sounds like man sana, man healthy, una manzana a day keeps the doctor away, ahhhggg, stop me!

Esperar is **to wait**, nothing to do with peras, pears. **Está esperando** = **is waiting**. Now try this question: ¿**hace mucho que usted espera?** That means **have you been waiting long?** Try it. ¿Hace mucho que usted espera?

Siempre means **always**. I think siempre might be a brand name for feminine hygiene products, so you will know what it means if you see it. **Siempre fui** = **I always was**, or I have always been. Siempre fui tu amigo. **I have always been me** = **siempre fui yo**.

Una pregunta is **a question**, any question, not just a question that you ask of your German friend, Gunter. Una pregunta = a question. Now, see if you can understand the next chiste.

29

— Una manzana está esperando el autobús, con una banana.

— La banana pregunta, - ¿hace mucho que usted espera?

— La manzana responde, - no, yo siempre fui manzana.

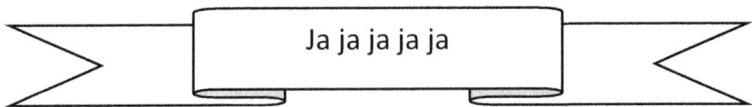

Ja ja ja ja ja

Now es hora to talk about the word como. **Como** means **I eat**. **Comida** is **food**, so you can say, come eata la comida. **Como** also means **how**. No es un chiste, pero es divertido to do an internet search on "how did that happen." Some of los imágenes son divertidos. En español, **how did it happen** is ¿**cómo pasó?** There is a long running telenovela, a historical soap opera about Spain during la dictadura de Franco, y se llama *Cuéntame como pasó*. If you search "como pasó" you tend not to get los imágenes divertidos; you tend to get imágenes de esa telenovela. It is good, by the way, and you can watch it online at rtve.es.

Como means **how**. **Como** means **I eat**. **Como** also means **like**, in the sense, soy como mi madre, I am like my mother. All this means, you can say, "how do I eat? I eat like I eat", all with the same word.

— ¿Cómo como?

— Como como como.

Use the Spanish

Ask for fruit

- Una manzana = an apple

- Una pera = a pear

- Una naranja = an orange

Talk to a friend

- Siempre fui tu amigo/ amiga = I have always
  been your friend

---

* * * * *

SOY = I AM

Soy means **I am**. Soy como mi madre means I am like my mother. Soy como mi madre in some ways; no soy como mi madre in others.

— Soy Milk, - just means, - I am milk.

Who are you, is **¿quién eres?** Remember, qu make a /k/ sound en español.

— ¿Quién eres?

— Soy Sauce.

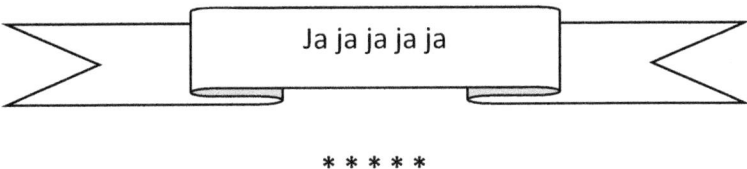

Ja ja ja ja ja

* * * * *

S.O.C.K.S. DELICIOSO

I hope you are getting to know un poco de español. Would you like to learn a nice little way to say, that really is fantastic, that really is delicious, or that really is horrible. No es difícil. Es fácil. **Fácil** means **easy**. En inglés facile means easily accomplished, or that someone has done something the easy way.

These next things you can learn are *SO* fáciles it is almost un chiste. To say, **that really is**, say, **eso sí que es** … **Eso** means **that**. **Sí** means **yes**. **Que es** means **that is**. **Eso sí que es** … means **that really is**… Then you can add fantástico, delicioso or horrible, pronounced /o-ree-blay/. The great thing about these sentences is they are easy to remember if you spell

32

out the word SOCKS. S.O.C.K.S. That sounds exactly like, eso sí que es. Isn't that great! S.O.C.K.S. fantástico. Eso sí que es fantástico.

Use the Spanish

Comment on your meal

- Eso sí que es delicioso = That really is delicious
- Eso sí que es horible = That really is horrible

---

* * * * *

EYES AND NOSES

We already found out that **cara** is **face** en español. Do you remember, **máscara o rímel** is the word for **mascara**, and it sort of masks your cara, your face.

Nose is **nariz**. To say **yes**, just say **sí**. To say **no**, just say **no**. But sometimes you don't know, so **I don't know** is **no sé**.

— How do you say nariz en inglés?
— No sé.

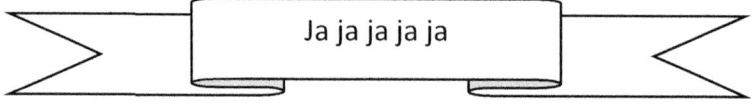

Ja ja ja ja ja

Eyes are **ojos**. You know that j makes a /h/ sound en español. Papá Noel says jo jo jo. So ojos are pronounced /ohos/. **Sobre** means **about**.

— Chistes sobre las narices stink.

— Pero chistes sobre los ojos are cornea.

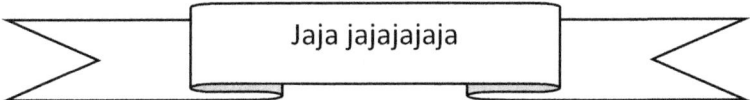

Jaja jajajajaja

Mucho de español es similar al inglés. Por ejemplo, we say **the tip of the iceberg** about something when we only know un poco about something that goes a lot deeper, y es igual en español. They say, eso es solo **la punta del iceberg**. It is paralelos como ese that make español fácil for English speakers.

Of course, mucho del vocabulario es similar, and that makes it easy too. Por ejemplo, **salad** is **ensalada**, and **lettuce** is **lechuga**. The words that are most común tend to be the most diferentes. Por ejemplo, **fue** is **he went**.

Duele means **it hurts**. La pronunciación es /dwelay/. Making a question, una pregunta, en español es fácil. You can just do it with el tono de voz. To ask, **does it hurt**, just say, ¿**duele?**

— Un hombre fue al doctor with some lechuga growing out of his nariz.

— El doctor pregunta, ¿duele?

— Sí, duele mucho. Eso es solo la punta del iceberg.

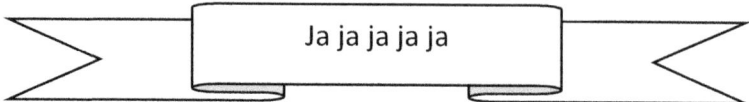

Ja ja ja ja ja

A couple of really important words are **house**, which is **casa**, and **money**, which is **dinero**. Casablanca is a city in Morrocco, North Africa, just across el Mediterraneo de España. **Casablanca** means **white house**. El Presidente de **Los Estados Unidos**, the States United or **the United States**, lives en la Casablanca. **Su casa** means **his house**, or **their house**.

Dinero means **money**. You could pay for your dinner with dinero. So Robert De Niro is nearly, but not quite, called Robert Money. **Su dinero** means **his money** or **their money**. **Tengo** means **I have**. **Los ojos** are **eyes** and **la nariz** is **the nose**.

— Tengo los ojos de mi madre, y la nariz de mi padre.

— En mi opinión my brother got the better deal. He got su casa y su dinero.

Nariz is **nose**. **Ojos** are **eyes**. **Cara** is **face** and **orejas** are **ears**. You say /o-re-has/. You might remember that **como** is **I eat** or **I am eating**. **You eat**, or **you are eating** is **comes**. To make it negative, you just say **no comes**. **Bien** means **well**, so to say **you are not eating well**, say **no comes bien**.

— Un hombre fue al doctor, con lechuga en la nariz y tomates en las orejas.

— El doctor took one look at him and said, - I can tell que no comes bien.

Use the Spanish

Talk about things that are important to you.

- Mi cara, mi nariz y mi voz = My face, my nose and my voice
- Mis ojos y mis orejas = My eyes and my ears
- Mi casa y mi dinero = My house and my money

---

* * * * *

ANIMALS, PARTICULARLY BEARS

Muchos animales en español are guessable if you speak inglés. Por ejemplo, I think you can guess what these animal words mean: chimpancé, gorila, orangután, jaguar, leopardo, león, pantera, tigre, chihuahua, canguro, koala, alpaca, búfalo, camello, jirafa, hámster, elefante, hipopótamo, rinoceronte, delfín, armadillo, hiena, panda, flamenco, pingüino, mosquito, piraña, salmón, sardina, escorpión, serpiente, anaconda, cobra, aligátor, tortuga y cocodrilo.

You might not be able to guess the word for **a bear** though; that's **un oso**. Ursa is the word for the bear constellations in the stars, and oso is a word that comes from the same Latin word that gave us Ursa Major and Ursa Minor. That might help you remember that un oso is a bear.

— What do you call an angry bear in Spanish?

— Un furioso.

— What do you call a chocolate bear in Spanish?

— Un delicioso.

— What do you call a glamorous bear in Spanish?

— Un fabuloso.

— What do you call a bear who has an affair with a politician in Spanish?

— Un escándaloso.

— What do you call an uneasy bear in Spanish?

— Un nervioso.

— What do you call a celebrity bear in Spanish?

— Un famoso.

— What do you call an expensive bear in Spanish?

— Un precioso.

— What do you call a multi-skilled bear in Spanish?

— Un talentoso.

Divertido is one word for **funny**, and **un chiste** is the word for **joke**. Another word for **funny** is **chistoso**, so what do you call a funny Spanish bear?

Use the Spanish

Call someone an animal

- Chimpancé = Chimpanzee

- Elefante = Elephant

- Tortuga = Tortoise

Use a describing word to pass judgement

- Es delicioso = It is delicious

- Es fabuloso = It is fabulous

- Es escándaloso = It is scandalous

---

* * * * *

SCHOOL

There are always muchos chistes about school, and one of the words for **school** en español is **escuela**, say /eskwela/. The **students** are los **estudiantes** or **alumnos** ... that is like our word **pupils**. The **teachers** are **los profesores** or **maestros**, and of course, we have the word maestro for someone who is very good at something, como el violín por ejemplo.

Cerrada means **closed**.

> — La maestra pregunta a Luis, - Luis, ¿Cómo te imaginas la escuela ideal?
> — Cerrada, maestra. Cerrada.

¿Por qué? means **why?** La pronunciación es /poor kay/. Funny thing is, **porque** means **because**, and it sounds the same. To help you remember, think of a woman called Kay. She is sad. Poor Kay! ¿Por qué es poor Kay sad? Porque she's not rich Kay. That can help your memoria: **¿Por qué? = Why? Porque = because.**

Hablar is **to talk**. The H is silent, so it sounds like /ablar/ and that makes me think of bla bla blar, which is a comment I might make if someone wouldn't stop talking. The verb changes slightly for different people, so **I talk** is **hablo**, and **you talk** is **hablas**.

— La maestra pregunta, - Luis, ¿Por qué hablas en mi clase?

— Luis responde, - maestra, ¿Por qué hablas en mi conversación.

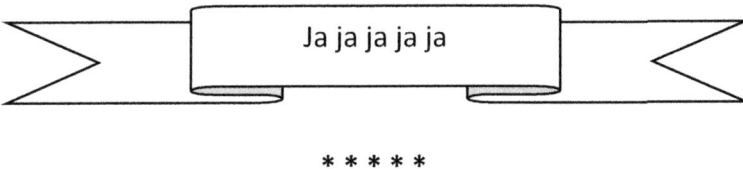

Ja ja ja ja ja

* * * * *

HOW MUCH?

It is useful to know how to ask for **a price**, **un precio**, and it´s quite nice en español. **How much** is **cuánto**, which has the ring of quantity to it, and quantity has to do with how much. **To cost** is **costar**, couldn't be simpler, but it costs es un poco diferente: **it costs** is **cuesta**. So **how much does it cost**, literally, how much it costs, is **¿Cuánto cuesta?**

In most Spanish speaking countries the "pennies" are cents: centímos or centavos. In some places it's pesos, but let's use el ejemplo de España, where **las monedas** or **coins** are Euros y centímos.

Then if you decide el precio está bien, you might say, **I'll buy it**: **lo compro**.

— Un niño gets on to un autobús. He asks the driver,
- ¿cuánto cuesta el autobús?

— Un euro y diez centímos.

— Lo compro. Everybody off!

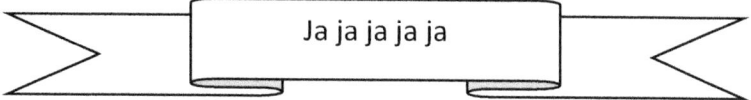

Ja ja ja ja ja

The Spanish word **estufa** means **heater**. It sounds similar to estafa, meaning a **swindle** or **scam**. There was **a film, una película**, called Ocean's Eleven. I wish it was called Ocean's Once en español, porque that would make the word once, /on-say/, easier to remember. Pero no. En español se llama La gran estafa. It helps now that I want you to remember that **estafa** means **swindle** or **scam**, and remember that **estufa** is a **heater**.

— ¿Cuánto cuesta esta estufa?

— Cinco mil dólares ($5000).

— ¡Esto es una estafa!

— No, señor, esto es una estufa.

* * * * *

WHAT IS THE DIFFERENCE

There are some things that we say differently en inglés compared to how we say them en español. I know they are lenguajes diferentes, I know. What I mean is, por ejemplo, en inglés we say **what is the difference**. En español we say **cuál es la diferencia**, literally, which is the difference. You understand now? Es un poco diferente.

Do you remember how to say nariz en inglés? **Sí** would be **yes**. **No** would be **no**. And if you don't know, it's no sé. No sé is a useful thing to know. You might need to say **I don't know** to someone que no habla inglés when you are on holiday en España o México, and now you can! **No sé.**

42

I don't care is **no me importa**. I want you to enjoy reading about español, y no me importa if you don't estudiar y memorizar every last word. No me importa.

— ¿Cuál es la diferencia entre la ignorancia y la apatía?

— No sé, y no me importa.

Use the Spanish

Comment on your own state

- No sé = I don't know

- No me importa = I don't care

---

* * * * *

UNA SERPIENTE

A snake is **una serpiente**. En inglés we would say how long something is, pero en español we say how long something measures. Por ejemplo, yo mido **un metro setenta, one metre seventy**.

— Mi serpiente mide exactamente tres coma uno cuatro metros. 3.14 metros. He's a πthon.

A short snake is **una serpiente corta**.

— When will la serpiente corta arrive?

— No sé, but he won't be long.

Un tipo de serpiente is a cobra, but **cobrar** means **to charge**, as in to ask for money for something. **Cobra** without the final -r is **he charges** or **she charges**.

— Help, el serpiente bit me!

— ¿Cobra?

— No, gratis.

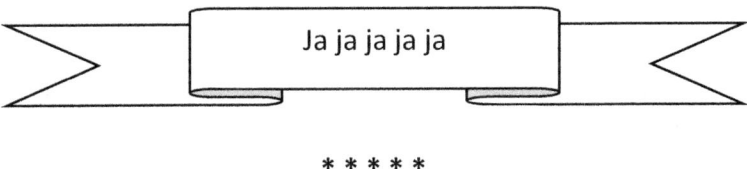

Ja ja ja ja ja

* * * * *

MY BRAIN = MI CEREBRO

I am interested in how we learn. **I think** is **pienso**; **to think** is **pensar**. In English, you are pensive when you are feeling thoughtful. **The brain** is **el cerebro**. En inglés, the cerebellum is part of the brain; en español el cerebro is the whole thing.

Pienso is **I think**. If you want to say **I used to think**, you say **solía pensar**. If you want to say you **used to** do anything, just use **solía** then the verb.

— Solía pensar que el cerebro es el órgano más importante.

— Then I thought, look what's telling me that.

Mi mente is **my mind**. **De mente** is **of the mind**, which makes me wonder if that is where we get the word demented from.

— I wasn't going to get un trasplante de cerebro, but then I changed mi mente.[1]

* * * * *

SEEING, LOOKING AND MIRRORS

The word for **eyes** is **ojos**. It sounds like this: /ohos/. We are learning a few words relacionado to the body. **Orejas** are **ears**, and nariz is … I forget. No sé.

To look is **mirar**, which I think sounds a bit like mirror. **Miras** is **you look**, which I think sounds a bit like mirrors. You look

---

[1] Changed my mind in Spanish is cambié de opinión, but sometimes you have to cambiar el lenguaje un poco to make el chiste funciona.

in a mirror, so I think that is a conexión that you can use to help la memoria. **You look closely** is **miras de cerca**, porque **cerca** is **close**.

Mirror is **espejo**. Say, /es-pe-ho/. The roots of the words espejo and mirror are clearly differentes. Espejo is closer in its origin to spectacles, and both espejo and spectacles help you see.

To look like something is **parecer**. Parecer is to look like or to seem to be. **Puede** is **it can**. **Puede parecer** means **it can look like**. Por ejemplo, puede parecer ciencia ficción, pero este es tu futuro; puede parecer un poco diferente; puede parecer chistoso. El verbo changes a bit, depending on the subject. **I seem** is **parezco**. **You seem** is **pareces**. **They seem** is **parecen**.

— When you get close, y miras de cerca, todos, and I mean all … todos los espejos parecen ojos.

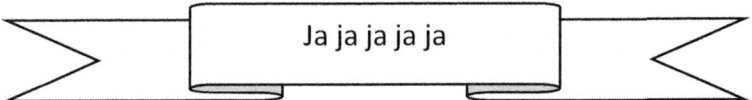
Ja ja ja ja ja

To see is **ver**. Remember, en español the letter v often sounds like a /b/, so to see can sound like /ber/. **You see** is **ves**, sounding like /bes/.

— Pienso que I would like a job cleaning los espejos.

— It's just something I could realmente verme, see myself doing.

Use the Spanish

Talk about thinking

- Yo pienso = I think

- En mi opinión = In my opinion

- Solía pensar = I used to think

---

* * * * *

YOU CAN!

Puede is **it can**. **Puedes** is **you can**.

— ¿Por qué no puedes ver los elefantes, hiding in the trees?

— Porque they are really good at it.

Puedo is **I can**. Try to remember, **I can** is **puedo**; **you can** is **puedes**; **it can** is **puede**.

Espera means **wait**. You can use that before you say something divertido or chistoso. The word for **girlfriend** is **novia**, and because the letter v sounds like a /b/, la

47

pronunciación de novia … espera … is /nob-ya/. **To change** is **cambiar**. Puedes cambiar novia to the word for boyfriend by making the -a into an -o. **Boyfriend** is **novio**, /nob-yo/.

— Mi novia told me she was leaving me porque I keep pretending to be a Transformer.

— I said no, espera. Puedo cambiar.

Use the Spanish

Talk about abilities

- (No) puedes ver = You can (not) see
- (No) puedo ver = I can (not) see

＊ ＊ ＊ ＊ ＊

SAINTS

The Spanish word for **saint** is **san**. **San Francisco** actually means **Saint Frances**. **San José** is **Saint Joseph**, and is the name for the capital city of Costa Rica, a beautiful country full of rain forest and beaches in Central America. **San Miguel** is **Saint Michael** … we name churches after San Miguel en **Inglaterra** (that's the word for **England**). En España, San Miguel is a beer!

— Do you know who the patron saint of shoes is en
   España?
— San Dalia.

* * * * *

COGNATES AND FALSE FRIENDS

Lots of Spanish words are very similares a sus equivalentes
ingleses, but not all words that look similares mean what
you might expect them to. **Sopa** is **soup**, and **soap** is **jabón**.
Ropa is **clothes**, and **rope** is **cuerda**. **Mantequilla**, /man-
tay-keel-ya/ is **butter**.

— Sopa is not soap. Ropa is not rope. And butter is
   not meant-to-kill-ya.

You have to be careful con español. Sometimes the words
you think you understand mean something quite diferente
to what you expect. Por ejemplo, you might think that the
word embarazada means embarrassed. But no! When you
tell people, **soy embarazada**, you are saying, **I am pregnant**.
Not quite the same, although it could be an embarrasing
error. There are plenty more!

— A mocha coffee, is what I wanted to say.

— But I said, dame un café de moco.

— This sentence caused a few giggles. ¿Por qué?

— The word **moco** means **snot**!

Conocerte means **to meet you**. For another ejemplo, imagine you meet a Spanish speaker, and you want to try out your charm, so you say, es un delito conocerte. Delito looks like our word delight. Unfortunately, the real meaning is crime, so **es un delito conocerte** means **it is a crime to meet you**. You might be better off saying, es un placer conocerte. **Placer** means **pleasure**.

Of course, it works the other way too. Spanish speakers can get words mixed up. If you **have a cold**, en español, you are **constipado**. A Spanish speaker who askes for some tissue, "because I am constipated," might raise a few eyebrows.

Use the Spanish

Meet someone, and tell them some news!

- Es un placer conocerte = It is a pleasure to meet you
- Soy embarazada = I am pregnant

50

UN OSO EN UN BAR

Pedir means **to ask for**. **He asks for** is **pide**, pronounced /peeday/. **I ask for** is **yo pido**, pronounced /yo peedo/, which sounds a bit unfortunate, en mi opinión.

A bartender or **a waiter** is **un camarero** if it is a man, or **una camarera** if it is a woman. I like to imagine that my waiter is called Cameron and comes from Cameroon.

— Un oso entra un bar, y pide al camarero, - un whisky y una ……………………………. Coca Cola por favor.
— ¿Por qué the big pause? Asked el camarero.
— No sé, shrugged el oso. I was born with them.

Yo means **I** or **me**. **Tú** means **you**. So I am a yo yo, and you are a tutu.

> You could do a really cute drawing of a yo yo and a tutu meeting, with speech bubbles saying "yo yo", and "tú tú". Yo = I; tú = you.

* * * * *

LOS NÚMEROS

Con means **with**, and **sin** means **without**. Con is easy to remember. **Chili con carne** means **chili with meat**. **Contexto** means **context**, but you might be able to see how contexto could mean with text. Sin es más difícil, porque sin in English is an offence against religious law. Jesús (Spanish pronunciación /hay-soos/) said, "Let he who is without sin throw the first stone." He who is sin sin ...

The word **dice** means **he says**, or **she says**. I think dice sounds a little bit like "he say" ... la pronunciación is /dee-say/. **¿Qué dice?** That means what does he say, literally **what he say**. Do you know los números? 0 is cero. Then it's uno, dos, tres, cuatro, cinco, seis, siete, ocho, nueve, diez. **A hundred** is **cien**, like the brand of **soap**, **jabón**.

— ¿Qué dice diez a cero?

— To be like you, I'd have to be sincero.

Ropa means **clothes**. **Un cinturón** is **a belt**.

— ¿Qué dice cero a ocho?

— Bonito cinturón.

Un sombrero is **a hat**. **Una corbata** is **a tie**.

— ¿Qué dice el sombrero a la corbata?

— You hang around, I'll go on ahead.

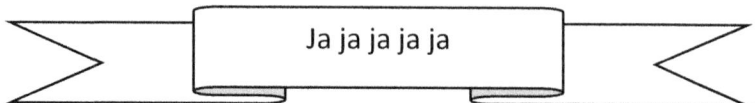

Ja ja ja ja ja

The word for **how many** is **cuántos**. It sounds like quantity, so it kind of makes sense. **Times** is **veces**. **One time** is **una vez**, and **many times** is **muchas veces**.

— ¿Cuántas veces can you subtract diez from cien?

— Una vez. After that you would be subtracting from ninety.

I like los números from sixteen to twenty. **Sixteen** is **dieciséis**, and that sounds like diez y seis, ten and six. It also sounds like "dee ez ee says" or "do as he says" in the regional acento, Geordie, from el norte de Inglaterra. **Seventeen** is **diecisiete**, diez y siete, ten and seven; **eighteen** is **dieciocho**, diez y ocho, ten and eight, eighteen; then it's diecinueve and **twenty** is **veinte**.

Veinte sounds like vente, which is what you would say to un amigo who you want to come with you.

Con means **with**. With me is a single word though. It is nice. **Conmigo** is **with me**, and **contigo** is **with you**. **Vente conmigo** means **come with me**. It sounds just like **veinte conmigo**, **twenty with me**.

— ¿Qué dice dieciocho a dos?
— Vente conmigo.

We have had a look at a few números, and you might know that en español, when you say how old you are, you use tengo, I have. Por ejemplo, **yo tengo veintiún años** ... that means I have twenty-one years, or **I am twenty-one**.

We are all getting older, or at least, ese es el plan. **Sixty** is **sesenta**. **Seventy**, **setenta**. Let's practicar unos números, counting from sesenta, sixty, in fives to one hundred. Sesenta, sesenta y cinco. Setenta, setenta y cinco. Ochenta, ochenta y cinco. Noventa, noventa y cinco, y cien.

Do you have grandparents? Your **grandad** is your **abuelo**, pronunciado /abwelo/. Your **gran** es tu **abuela**, /abwela/. To ask how old someone is, you say **how many years he or she has**, like this: **¿Cuántos años tiene?** ¿Cuántos años tiene tu abuelo? Mi abuelo tiene setenta años (70). ¿Cuántos años tiene tu abuela? Sesenta y cinco (65). **Tenía** is **she had**, so I can say mi abuela tenía veinte años when she got married.

Cuando is the word for **when.** Look up the Italian/ English song, *Quando, Quando, Quando.* Quando means when in italiano. **Tenía** is **she had**, remember. Mi abuela tenía veinticinco años cuando tenía mi madre.

What is the English for nariz? No sé. The word for **now** is **ahora**. I like that ahora contains the word **hora**, which means **hour** or **time**, and **ahora** means **now.**

— Cuando mi abuela tenía sesenta años el doctor le recomendó that she walk cinco kilómetros every day.

— Ahora mi abuela tiene ochenta y cinco años y no sé dónde está, where she is.

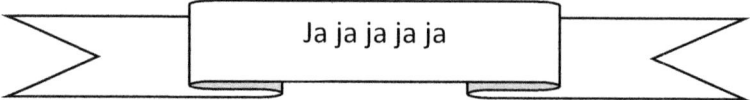

Ja ja ja ja ja

Ahora is a word used to talk about el presente. Los verbos en inglés, y en español, can be changed a little bit to make them talk about el pasado, like **tengo** is **I have**, and **tenía** is **I had**. Those differences are called **tense, tenso** en español. Like they **enter** is **entran**, and they **entered** is **entraron.**

Present tense and **past** tense. Or, otro ejemplo, **es** means **it is**, and **era** means **it was**. **Presente** y **pasado**.

— El futuro, el presente y el pasado entraron un bar.

— Era tenso.

Use the Spanish

Buy some clothing

- Un sombrero = A hat

- Un cinturón = A belt

- Una corbata = A tie

Invite your grandparente

- Vente conmigo, abuela = Come with me, Gran

- Vente conmigo abuelo = Come with me, Grandad

---

* * * * *

LOS NIÑOS = THE KIDS

To ask **where is she** or **where is he**, say **¿dónde está?** To ask **where are they**, it's **¿dónde están?** One of the Spanish words for **darling** is **cariño**.

— Cariño, ¿dónde están los niños?

— En inglés.

— Buf! Where are the kids?

Los niños means **the children**, of course.

En español a **full stop** or a **dot** is **un punto.** A **comma** is **una coma.** **To eat** is **comer,** and in English, comestibles are things you eat, although comestibles isn't a very commonly used word. **Vamos a** means **we are going to.**

— Vamos a comer niños.

— Vamos a comer, niños.

— Comas. They save lives.

* * * * *

GRACIAS

It is good to know your pleases and thank yous in any lenguaje that you are going to be using. **Please** is **por favor,** and **thank you** is **gracias. Word** is **palabra** en español. I think of the parables de la Biblia, stories to illustrate a moral point. **The word of God,** some say. **La palabra de Dios. Explicar** means **to explain,** y yo pienso that it is good to explicar las palabras.

— Gracias por explicarme la palabra mucho. It means a lot.[2]

Muchas gracias means **thanks a lot**. Imagine un amigo pushing you so you slide down a big grassy bank on your bottom, and you stain the seat of your trousers green. What would you say to your amigo? Gracias for the grassy ass!

You might remember that **abuela** means **grandma**. Mi abuela does loads of sit-ups, and she has great abs. Ab-wella-wella-a!

Navidad is the word for **Christmas**. It's a bit like nativity, navidad. Mi abuela gave the best presents for navidad, she gave me un cheque. The thing with un cheque is it needs a signature. You might think that signature would be asignatura en español, pero no. **Asignatura** is a **school subject**, like las matemáticas, el inglés o las ciencias, and **firmar** is **to sign**.

---

[2] I hope you don't mind if I repeat myself. I forget what I have said, and when I say the same chiste again, it helps me to remember!

- Mi madre decidió, un año, that she wasn't going to nag us to write cartas to say gracias for our gifts.
- Como resultado, mi abuela no recibió una carta to say gracias por el cheque generoso that she gave me.
- El próximo año, I went round in person the next day to say gracias. ¿Por qué?
- Porque mi abuela no firmó el cheque.

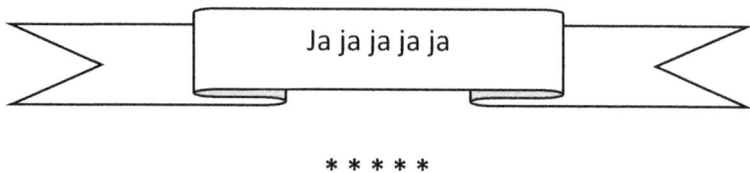

Ja ja ja ja ja

* * * * *

RELATIONSHIPS

I love the word for **relationship** en español: **compromiso**. **Compromiso** can mean an **engagement**, a **date**, or in a non-romantic sense, an **obligation**. A compromise en inglés, means an agreement when the people involved reduce their demands, o cambian sus opiniones, so that they can agree.

Pienso means **I think**. When we are pensive we are thoughtful, so pienso and I think have that conexión. Pienso que **puedo crear, I can create**, un diagrama de Venn to show the meanings of compromise en inglés, y compromiso en español, y la parte en el centro, donde las definiciones coinciden, would representar a dos personas, both of whom are not getting what they want.

En español,   **a compromise** is **una transigencia**, or **una solución intermedia.**

— La solución intermedia is we'll do it my way, and you'll find una manera to be okay con eso.

A couple is **una pareja**. The J makes that pronunciación, /pa-re-ha/. J is not the only way to make a /h/ sound en español. The letters GE make a /he/ sound, and GI make a /hee/ sound.   General is pronunciado /heneral/ and la palabra for **giant** is **gigante**, /hee-gan-tay/. **A gym** is **un gimnasio**, /him-na-sio/. En general, los gigantes visitan los gimnasios mucho.

Visitan means **they visit.** **They go** is **van**, and again, it often sounds like /ban/, porque la letter V makes a /b/ sound en español. I remember being at a festival and hearing un hombre español complementing un amigo on his converted horsebox. "I like your ban," the Spanish man said. Just to repeat, **van** en español means **they go**.

— Unas parejas no van al gimnasio. ¿Por qué?

— Porque not all compromisos work out.

Use the Spanish

Talk about your partner

- Tengo compromiso = I have a relationship
- Este es mi pareja = This is my partner

---

* * * * *

LAS CIENCIAS

En la escuela there are three asignaturas in the general categoria de las ciencias: la biología, la física y la química. Biología is pronounced /bee-o-lo-hia/, because GI make a /hee/ sound. **Química** es la palabra for **chemistry**, and the QU make a /k/ sound, so you say /kimica/. Física is easy to say, although for me, la física era la ciencia más difícil.

La química is about los elementos, la energía (say /ener-hia/), y las reacciones. **La vida** means **life**. Ricky Martin is living **la vida loca, the crazy life**. La biología es la ciencia de la vida. La física, no sé. I don't know. ¿La física es la electricidad, el movimiento, la radiación, la gravedad y las matemáticas? No sé. It's not about noses, that's all I know!

Muchas de las palabras en las ciencias son iguales en inglés y en español. ¿Comprendes? A lot of the words in science are the same (equal, iguales) in English and Spanish. Everyday words can be very diferentes, like **calle** = **street**; **caminaban** = **walking**; **detente** = **stop**; and **pregunta** = **question**. Pero las palabras de las ciencias are often very similares.

— Un protón y un neutrón caminaban por la calle.

— El protón dice, - Detente, I've dropped un electrón. Help me look for it.

— El neutrón pregunta, - Are you sure?

— El protón responde, - Sí, soy positivo.

The word for **it has** is **tiene**, y la pronunciación es perfecta if you say the letters t.n.a. I like to think about what DNA tiene … DNA tiene el codigo genético, say, /henetico/. (I love hens! I have a chicken called Tina. I love our hen Tina. She does a little tango dance move, and I wonder if she is from Argentina. Guess how to pronounce Argentina en español! /Ar-hen-tina/. I really do love our hen Tina).

To get the last chiste, about el protón y el neutrón, you need to know that un protón tiene **una carga, a charge**, positiva; un neutrón no tiene una carga, y un electrón tiene una carga negativa. You know that, so you understand el chiste.

Do you remember la palabra **chiste**? It means **joke**. I hope estos chistes are helping you to learn un poco de español. **Todos** means **all**. **No sé** means **I don't know**, so what do you think sé, on its own, means? **Sé** means **I know**. Sé is pronounced /say/. Sé que no todos los chistes funcionan.

— I'd tell you un chiste de química, pero sé that I wouldn't get una reacción.

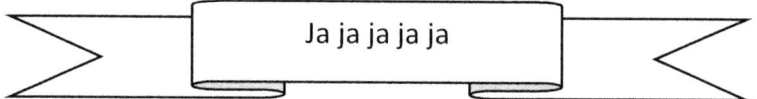
Ja ja ja ja ja

Las palabras en las ciencias often come from Latin, porque Latin was el lenguaje de la educación cuando la educación comenzó en Inglaterra, y español is a direct descendant of Latin, gracias a los Romanos. We talk about reacciones en la química. **It reacts** is **reacciona**. You see, they are really very similares.

Do you remember la palabra for waiter or barman? Imagina que es un hombre llamado Cameron y that he comes from Cameroon. The word for **here** is **aquí**. La pronunciación is /a-key/, like do you have a key for here? And do you remember the word for **he says**? I think it sounds a bit like **he says**. It is **dice**, /dee-say/.

— Helium entra en un bar.
— El camarero dice, - Aquí no servimos gases nobles.
— El helio no reacciona.

I like un chiste que tiene una formula, porque it is nice to know what to expect. I like set pieces of diálogo too. When you talk to un camarero, you might expect to ask how much it costs, and that is all good Spanish. The word for **how much** is **cuánto**, related to quantity. The word for **it costs** is **cuesta**. ¿Cuánto cuesta? You can use that when you go on vacation, de vacaciones, when you buy a drink. You can say drink, pero yo prefiero la palabra beverage. Check out the song, *Cold Beverage* by *G. Love & Special Sauce*. La palabra for **beverage** en español is **bebida**.

— Un neutrón entró en un bar y preguntó,
— ¿Cuánto cuesta una bebida?
— El camarero respondió, - para ti, sin cargo.

La **física** is **physics**. **Un físico** is a **physicist**. **La ciencia** is **science**, y **un científico** is a **scientist**. **La biología** is **biology** and **a biologist** is **un biólogo**. **La química** is **chemistry** and **a chemist** is **un químico**.

I already said, I like un chiste que tiene una formula. I like lightbulb jokes. **A lightbulb** is **una bombilla**. It is a nice word, and the double LL gives a /y/ sound: /bom-beeya/.

— ¿Cuántos físicos se necesitan para cambiar una bombilla?

— Dos. Uno to hold la bombilla, y otro to turn el universo.

Yo means **I**, and **tú** means **you**. Remember, a yo yo is a me me, and a tú tú is a you you.

Yo mencioné earlier that qu makes a /k/ sound. There are unas palabras that I really like with the /k/ sound. I like the word for **makeup**, **maquillaje**. Say /maky-yahey/. I also like the word for **luggage**, which is **equipaje**. Say /ekky-pahey/. **Your luggage** is **su equipaje**. **Tengo** is **I have**, so **tengo mucho equipaje** means **I have a lot of luggage**.

— Un fotón se registra en un hotel.

— La recepcionista pregunta, - Can I help you con su equipaje?

— El fotón responde, - no tengo equipaje. I'm travelling light.

Use the Spanish

Talk about learning a language

- Muchas palabras = A lot of words

- No era difícil = It wasn't difficult

- El lenguaje de la educación = The language of education

- No todos funcionan = They don't all work

- Soy positivo/ positiva = I am positive

---

* * * * *

LA GRAMÁTICA

No me importa means **I don't care.** It is not important to me. No me importa el estudio de la gramática, at least, not much. Prefiero el vocabulario. **Consolar** is to **console** or to comfort. **Consuelas** is **you comfort**, or with rising intonación, do you comfort. The word for **how** is **como.**

Como also means **I eat**. **Como** also means **like**. Do you remember this one:

— ¿Cómo como?

— Como como como.

So to say, **how do you comfort** is **¿cómo consuelas?** Pero si dices "¿cómo consolar?" instead, no me importa. El vocabulario comes first, second and third para mi. La gramática comes after that. Some people like la gramática, and give it mucho más importancia. They get upset si usas la puntuación con errores.

— ¿Cómo consuelas a un pedante de la gramática?

— There, their, they're.

En español we don't use the apostrophe mucho. Es usado in foreign words that are borrowed, y nombres, como McDonald's. En español, el apostrofo no se usa para indicar la posesión. Instead we say, por ejemplo, **la amiga de mi madre, the friend of my mother**. En inglés we can have a string of possession: **my mum's friend's son's teacher**. En español we can do that too, it just goes the other way round, y sin apóstrofos: **el profesor del hijo de la amiga de mi madre**.

Of course, el apóstrofo es importante en inglés y está bien saber un poco de la gramática.

— La gramática es la diferencia entre knowing your shit and knowing you're shit.

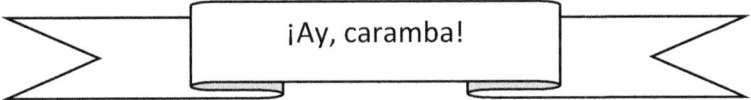

¡Ay, caramba!

Tiene means **it has**. El español no tiene el apóstrofo, pero sí tiene la coma. **Una coma** is **a comma**. **Una coma** is also **a coma**, un estado of extreme unresponsiveness, pero yo no sé un chiste that plays with the double meaning of una coma. **Como** means **I eat**, or **I am eating**. You remember ab-wela-wela ... gran!

— La importancia de la coma:

— Como abuela.

— Como, abuela.[3]

Use the Spanish

Say how you feel

- No me importa = I don't care
- Prefiero conversaciones = I prefer conversations

---

[3] I hope you don't mind if I repeat myself. I forget what I have said, and when I say the same chiste again, it helps me to remember!

LA CULTURA

Learning español is what we do so we can have conversaciones with people from other parts of the world. We use our knowledge of el lenguaje to find out más sobre la cultura.

— Spanish singer Alejandro Sanz was on la televisión with British TV host, Anne Diamond when he used the word mañana.

— Anne asked him to explain what it meant.

— Alejandro said that mañana means, - maybe the job will be done tomorrow, maybe the next day, maybe the day after that. Perhaps next week, next month, next year. Who cares?

— Anne turned to Irishman Shay Brennan who was also on the show, and asked if there was an equivalent in Irish.

— No. In Ireland we don't have a word to describe that level of urgency – replied Shay.

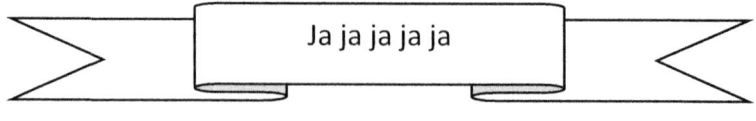

Ja ja ja ja ja

* * * * *

RELOJES = WATCHES

The J has a /h/ sound, so say /re-lo-hes/. **Relojes** means **watches** and it also means **clocks**. If you listen to Manu Chao's song, *Me Gustas Tu* you will hear someone telling the time. The chorus asks, **what time is it, my heart, ¿qué hora son, mi corazón?** At the end of the song you will hear someone say – radio reloj. La hora es un tema in that song. Can you remember the word for watches? The word for stolen is easy: **robada**. It's like **robbed**.

— Mi colección de relojes suizos fue robada en España.

— Adiós Omegas.

Telling the time en español es fácil. **Las dos, is two o' clock. Las tres** is **three o' clock**, and so on. **Y cuarto** means **quarter past**, and **y media** is **half past**.

— Las seis y media is the best time on un reloj.

— Hands down.

Your **waist** is your **cintura**, and a **belt** is un **cinturón**.

— I tried to make un cinturón out of relojes, but it was a waist of time.

En inglés, we say I am hungry. En español, we say **I have hunger**, and that is **tengo hambre**. **Are you hungry** is **¿tienes hambre? I was hungry** could be used as una excusa for having eaten something, and you say that like this: **tenía hambre. He or she was hungry** is just the same: **tenía hambre.**

— Did you hear about el reloj que tenía hambre?

— It went back four seconds.

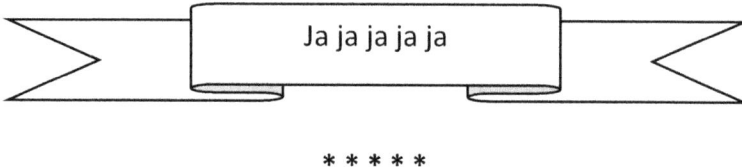

Ja ja ja ja ja

* * * * *

SPIDERS

A spider is **una araña**. I like the word, and if they are big enough, I like la creatura. I don't like spider mites, porque they attack my chickens, and our hen Tina doesn't like that.

La palabra for fear of spiders is **arachnophobia, aracnofobia** en español. Muchas palabras are very similares. **An anorak** is **un anorak**. En español we don't say, I am frightened, we say, **I have fear: tengo miedo.**

71

— Un amigo tiene miedo de arañas wearing raincoats.

— Anoraknafobia.

Las arañas comen moscas. That means **spiders eat flies.** It is easy to remember that **moscas** means **flies**, because **a little fly** is **un mosquito.**

You might know the word **ropa** means **clothes**, and **cinturón** means **belt.** **Pantalones** are **trousers.** **Silk** is **seda.** Imagina having pantalones made of seda de araña, spider silk!

— Tengo pantalones nuevos, made of seda de araña.

— They look bonitos, but the flies keep getting stuck.

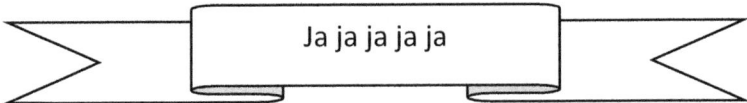
Ja ja ja ja ja

We live is **vivimos.** The letter V makes a /b/ sound so it sounds like /be-be-mos/. **Vivir** means **to live**, and that sounds like an instruction to be beer … but I don't want to be beer, because then I would get drunk! But I do want to vivir! What a dilema!

Vivimos con arañas. Some people kill them. Some people catch them and put them out en el jardín. **The rent** is el **alquiler.** It can be a killer, el alquiler.

72

Money is **dinero.** **A garden is un jardín,** and **a gardener** is **un jardinero.** That must be hard dinero.

Sí means **yes,** and **si** means **if.** Vitamin C is Spanish for vitamin yes. **Qué pasa** means **what happens, what if** or **what's up.** It is nice to ask un amigo, ¿qué pasa?

— ¿Qué pasa si el dinero that we randomly find en el sofá, if from las arañas, trying to pay el alquiler?

Unas personas tienen miedo de arañas = some people are afraid of spiders. En algunos lugares todo el mundo tiene miedo de arañas = in some places everyone is afraid of spiders.

— En Irán, todo el mundo tiene miedo de arañas.
— Pero en Iraq … no phobia.

Use the Spanish
Talk about feelings

- ¿Qué pasa? = What's up?
- Tengo hambre y tengo miedo = I'm hungry and frightened
- Y tengo muchos años = And I am very old

MI PAPA

Español es **divertido**. Español es **chistoso**. Español is **funny**.

Mi papá means **my dad**. As you might know, to say how old someone is en español, you say, por ejemplo, my dad has forty seven years. You might also know, that **año** means **year**, and **ano** means **anus**.

— Mi papá tiene cuarenta y siete años = my dad is 47 years old.

Una papa, sin el acento en la letra -a, means **a potato**.

— Mi papa tiene cuarenta y siete anos = my potato has 47 anuses.

El Papa, with a capital letter, means **the pope**.

— Mi Papa tiene cuarenta y siete anos = my pope has 47 anuses.

To laugh is **reir**. Reir es importante, but if I have offended you, perdón.

* * * * *

WORK

La palabra for **work** is **trabajo**, and you say /tra-ba-ho/. Imagina the seven dwarves from Snow White singing. – Hi ho, hi ho. It's off to work we go. – You could cambiarlo un poco: - Hi ho, hi ho. It's off to trabajo.

A job is un trabajo. I work is yo trabajo.

— I lost mi trabajo en el banco on my first day.

— Una señora asked me to check her balance.

— So I pushed her over.

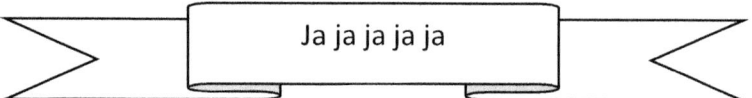

Ja ja ja ja ja

I like the word for **factory** en español. It's una **fábrica**, and of course it's where we produce, or fabricate things. Another meaning of fabricate is to invent something false to deceive someone. Does that mean that un trabajo en una fábrica is not a good, honest job?

To think is **pensar**, but another way to comunicar the same idea is to **believe, creer**. You might remember that **puedo** is **I can**, so **I can't believe** is **no puedo creer**.

— No puedo creer that I lost mi trabajo en la fábrica de calendarios. All I did was take a day off.

To get un trabajo, or un empleo as it is also known, you might have to have an interview. En español, **interview** is **entrevista**. The entre part is like inter, and the vista part is like view. Una de las preguntas que no me gustan is when I am asked to talk about mis errores, or about my worst qualities. **Malo** is **bad**, and **peor** is the word for **worst**. **Cualidad** is **quality**, so **my worst quality** es **mi peor cualidad**. **Demasiada** is **too**, like too much. See if you can understand el próximo chiste. Remember, **jefe** /hefay/, means **boss**.

— Un hombre va a una entrevista de trabajo con el jefe.
— El jefe pregunta, ¿Cuál es tu peor cualidad?
— El hombre dice, - probablemente soy demasiado honesto.
— El jefe dice, - pienso que ser honesto no es malo.
— El hombre responde, - no me importa lo que tú pienses.

No me importa clearly means **I don't care**. **No me importa** also means **I don't mind**, and **I don't like** is **no me gusta**. To go = **ir**. It sounds like ear. Ireland is Irlanda, and that sounds like Ear-Landa. They must like listening there. To go to Ireland sounds like this: ear a Ear-Landa. Would you like to ear a Ear-Landa? I know eye would.

I was talking about **trabajo, work**.

— No me importa ir a mi trabajo.

— Es solo que no me gustan las ocho horas I have to wait before I can go home again.

Use the Spanish

Talk about work experiences

- Mi trabajo no es malo = My work isn't bad
- No puedo creer mi jefe = I can't believe my boss
- Mi entrevista fue mala = My interview was bad

---

* * * * *

REST

To sleep is **dormir**. It's nothing like sleep, but it is like dormitory.

— Sometimes I Wake Up Grumpy.

— Other Times, I Let Her Dormir.

Awake is **despierto**, or if you are female, **despierta**. Normalmente, I am despierta during **el día, the day**, and I like to dormir **at night, de noche**. Sometimes I have insomnio, y no puedo dormir.

— I have been despierta toda la noche, trying to remember si tengo amnesia o insomnio.

Dormir is **to sleep**. **I will sleep** is **dormiré**. Spanish doesn't have a word for will. Instead you put something on the end of words that mean to something. **Ser** means **to be**, and **será** means **it will be**. ¡Qué será, será! That means **what will be, will be**. It's a song by Doris Day. Look it up, **it will help you, te ayudará**, to learn un poco de español. **Encontrar** means **to find**, so **I will find** would be **encontraré**. I think encontrar is similar to encounter, which is similar in meaning to find. **Hasta** means **until**, like hasta la vista, baby.

— No dormiré hasta encontrar una cura para mi insomnio.

It is nice to be comfortable cuando we go to bed to dormir. The word for **comfortable** is **cómodo**. We have the word commode, which means two things: a set of drawers is a commode, and a commode is also a type of toilet. So you could go to a commode to make yourself cómodo. Not in the drawers though!

Encontrar means **to find**, like to encounter, and cada means every.

— De noche no puedo encontrar una posición cómoda para dormir.

— Por la mañana cada posición es cómoda.

You **bed** is your **cama**. If you say **good night**, that is **buenas noches**. **Till tomorrow** is **hasta mañana**. **Mañana** is a funny word, porque it means **tomorrow** and it means **morning**, so **tomorrow morning** en español es: **mañana por la mañana**.

I like to remember la palabra cama with the tune to *Karma Chameleon,* the song by Culture Club.

— Cama cama cama cama cama ca- me lie on

— Lie on mi bed. Lie on mi bed, oh oh oh.

Your **dreams** are your **sueños**. Say /swenyos/. It is a nice word. You might have un sueño de noche, en tu cama. Tus sueños are also tus aspiraciones. Maybe you would like to **recibir dinero, to receive money** for what you like doing best. **Sueño** is also used to translate **sleep** sometimes.

To be is **ser**. Ser o no ser, esa es la pregunta. **Era** means it **was**. I think about how the 1960s *was* an *era* of sexo, drogas y rock and roll. **Un estudio** is **a study**. You can see la palabra study as parte de la palabra estudio. **Un estudiante** is a **student**. Estudiantes study **the day**, **el día**, **before**, **antes**. Estudia … día … antes. Estudiantes.

— Yo recibí dinero por ser parte de un estudio en la clínica del sueño.

— Era el trabajo de mis sueños.

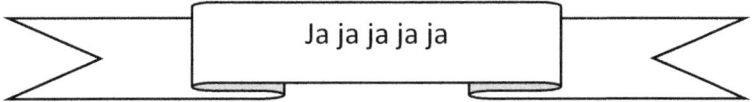

Ja ja ja ja ja

Dormir is **to sleep**, and **dormimos** is **we sleep**. Cuando dormimos, we sometimes **snore**, which is **roncar** en español. **You snore, my friend. Roncas, mi amigo.** The word for **easy** is **fácil**.

— Roncar es fácil para mí. I can do it in my sleep.

There is something automaticamente chistoso about snoring. **Mi abuelo** and **mi abuela** are **my grandparents, mis abuelos** en español. Mis abuelos roncaron tan fuerte, so loudly, that **they woke up other people in the hotel** when they were on holiday. Despertaron a las otras personas en el hotel cuando estaban de vacaciones.

— ¿Por qué las arañas "Black Widow" kill their mates after el sexo?

— To stop el ronquido before it starts.

Use the Spanish

Talk about sleep

- No puedo dormir = I can't sleep

- Tengo insomnio = I have insomnia

- Una posición cómoda en mi cama = a comfy position in my bed

- El ronquido = the snoring

---

* * * * *

PLAY

There are lots of games you can play using un poco de español. The word for **questions** is **preguntas**. I imagine mi amigo from Germany. Se llama Gunter. I imagine asking Gunter a question, and introducing my question with the words, pray, Gunter … The word for **play** is **jugar**. It's not at all similar to play, but looking at the word you could say es un poco similar a la palabra juggler, and juggling is almost playing. Juggling no es trabajo, in any case.

Puedes jugar veinte preguntas, using un poco de español. You have sí, no and no sé, and with veinte preguntas you have to guess what secret thing your opponent is thinking of, using preguntas that you answer only with sí and no.

Another thing que puedes jugar es **Simón dice**. That means **Simon says**. Just use Simón dice instead of introducing commands that must be obeyed with Simon says.

Jugar means **to play**, and **a game** is **un juego**. Mi juego favorito is an online puzzle que se llama **1010, diez diez**. I also like familias contentas, which is a bit like **go fish, ve pez** en español. **One fish** is **un pez**. **Two fish** are **dos peces**.

— ¿Cuál es el juego favorito de los peces?
— Salmón dice.

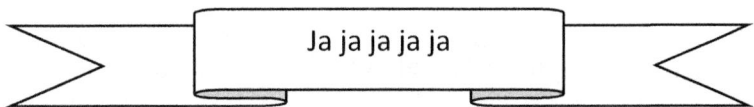
Ja ja ja ja ja

A king is **un rey** and **a queen** is **una reina**. To help la memoria, you could pensar en un rey reigning in a country; o, por ejemplo, we could talk about the reign of Reina

Victoria. There has to be un chiste with rain and reign. The word for **wet** is **mojado**. A mojito is a drink with rum, sugar, lime, mint and water, so I suppose un mojito is mojado. If you had a son, and he was little you could call him "mi hijo" or "mi hijito." If you threw a glass of water over him, you could call him "mi hijito mojado." If you threw a glass of mojito over him, you could call him "mi hijito mojito mojado."

There are two words that mean **was**: **era** and **estaba**. I am going to use estaba to say **he was wet**: **estaba mojado**.

— ¿Por qué estaba mojado el rey?
— He was the raining monarca.

The word for **chess** is **ajedrez**, which sounds a bit like a head dress. ¿Puedes imaginar a head dress? I can! Yo puedo imaginar un juego de ajedrez con todas la piezas wearing head dresses, like little **egipcios antiguos, ancient Egyptians** that is.

Many people piensan que el ajedrez es el rey de todos los juegos. **Me gusta** is **I like**, and **no me gusta** is **I don't like**. Personalmente, no me gusta el ajedrez. No me gusta pensar that much.

A dog is **un perro, una pera** is **a pear**, pero **una perra** is a **bitch**. Got that?

— En el parque, un señor juega al ajedrez con un perro.

— Tú perro es super inteligente, señor.

— No, realmente el perro no es super inteligente. I'm leading, tres juegos a uno.

It wouldn't be right to have una sección llamada PLAY sin uno o dos chistes sobre el fútbol. **A team** is **un equipo**. The QU make a /k/ sound, so it is less like equipment and more like /e-keep-o/. **Our team** is **nuestro equipo**, so **nuestro** means **our**: nuestro equipo.

The manager is **el jefe** or **el gerente**, and both of those words start with a /he/ sound. **Suportar** doesn't mean support, it means **to put up with**. **Mirar** is **to watch**. ¿Tú miras el fútbol?

— El nuevo gerente de nuestro equipo es estricto y no suporta any nonsense. Last Saturday he caught dos fanáticos climbing over the wall del estadio, y estaba furioso with them.

— ¡Get back in there y mira el juego hasta el final!

Life is **la vida**, and **death** is **la muerte**. **Day of the dead** is **día de los muertes**. After a person dies, and before they have their funeral, they go to the mortuary. Mortuary and muerte have a close conexión. Para unas personas el fútbol is a matter of la vida y la muerte. Para otras personas es más importante que eso.

One of the words for **maybe** en español is **quizás**. Because QU make a /k/ sound, that is /kis-ass/. Because there is un acento, the emphasis is on the ass. There is a great song by Andrea Boccelli called *Quizás, quizás, quizás*. It's worth a listen. Quizás you can learn to lip-sync to it.

After la muerte, quizás your soul goes to heaven or to hell. **Heaven** is **cielo** en español, and **hell** is **el infierno**. Cielo sounds like /see-yellow/. Si tu puedes pensar de una conexión between heaven and see yellow, let me know! **Dios** is **God**, and **Satanás** is **el diablo, the devil**. Hell is infernal, so infierno no es una palabra difícil. **Play** is **jugar**, and **a player** is **un jugador**. **A referee** is **un árbitro**, and the referees do do the arbitration, I suppose.

— Dios y el diablo were having an argument, y Satanás propuso un juego de fútbol entre el cielo y el infierno para resolver la disputa.

— Dios pointed out that it wouldn't be **un juego justo, a fair game**, porque todos los jugadores buenos go to el cielo.

— El diablo smiled y respondió: - sí, pero yo tengo todos los árbitros.

Use the Spanish

Deal with questions

- Sí. No. No sé. = Yes. No. I don't know.
- ¿Por qué? = Why?
- Porque = Because
- ¿Por qué no? = Why not?
- No me gustan preguntas = I don't like questions
- Es más importante que eso = It's more important than that
- No me gusta pensar = I don't like thinking

---

* * * * *

GOLDILOCKS

One of the most important things you can learn to say is that you don't understand. It isn't defeatist, it's practical. **I don't understand** = **no entiendo**. **He has** is **tiene**, and that sounds like T.N.A. **I understand** is **entiendo**, and that sounds like N.T.N.doh. Like dynamite. T.N.T. But inside out, and with a "doh" on the end: N.T.N.doh. So if that is I understand, **I don't understand** is **no entiendo**.

Goldilocks, la historia para niños, se llama **Ricitos de Oro** en español. Yo no entiendo Ricitos de Oro. La historia es que una familia de tres osos has made breakfast and then gone out for a walk, when Ricitos de Oro turns up, and has a taste of the three bowls of porridge.

Demasiado is **too**, as in **too much**. **Más** is **more**, and demasiado is like if we made the word "of-more-ied", something like that, en mi opinión. You know la historia de Ricitos de Oro, so you know that el vocabulario importante incluye **porridge**, **avena** en español; **hot**, which is **caliente**; and **cold**, which is **frío**. Pero yo no entiendo como una familia prepara su avena, serves it out into tres platos, and from one pan, on one ring on the hob, you get un plato de la avena que es demasiado caliente, un plato de la avena que es demasiado frío, y un plato de la avena que es perfecto. Y no entiendo por qué los osos go out, without having eaten la avena that someone ha preparado and that is ready for them on the breakfast table. No entiendo ese historia. Ricitos de Oro y los tres osos estúpidos. Perdone, Osos, pero yo sé that real life osos would never walk away from breakfast.

Use the Spanish

Communication

- Entiendo = I understand

- No entiendo = I don't understand

Talk about the weather

- Demasiado frío = Too cold

- Demasiado caliente = Too hot

---

* * * * *

LA FILOSOFÍA

Hay means **there is** or **there are**, and the H is mute, so it sounds like ay. **A glass** is **un vaso**, so **a glass of water** is **un**

vaso de agua, and **a glass of wine** is **un vaso de vino**. So there is a glass of water, is **hay un vaso de agua**.

An **engineer** is a nice word. **Ingeniero** is pronounced with a hen in the middle: /in-hen-yeah-row/. En inglés es una combinación interesante de palabras: in hen yeah row. I have been to a holiday park with a little lake, and you could get a boat shaped like a swan. It was peddle power. Un ingeniero could make a boat shaped like a hen that you had to row. Then you could say, get in hen, yeah, row! If you were de vacaciones con un ingeniero you could say that to el ingeniero.

Full is **lleno**. It sounds like yeah no: /ye-no/. **Empty** is **vacío**. It sounds like /ba-see-yo/, with the emphasis on the see. If Baz has un vaso vacío, and he looks through it at you, Baz see you through el vaso vacío. Will that help you remember? No sé.

Dicen means **they say**. **I say** is **digo**, and **he or she says** is **dice**. Dice, /dee-say/, sounds a bit like he say.

— Unas personas dicen que el vaso está medio lleno.

— Unas personas dicen que el vaso está medio vacío.

— Los ingenieros dicen que el vaso es dos veces más grande de lo necesario.

Eso es la filosofía.

Dijo means **he said** or **she said**. **Hazme** means **make me**. **Haz** means **make**, and the two words are stuck together: hazme. **Uno** means **one**. **Con todo** means **with everything**.

— Una buddista en una pizzería dijo:

— Hazme una con todo.

Eso es la filosofía.

Use the Spanish

Report speech

- Dijo = He said
- Dicen = They said

---

* * * * *

EXERCISE = EXERCISE

One of my favourite Spanish words is ejercicio, because it sounds so Spanish. I don't usually lisp. The sounds that get lisped, en unas partes de España, are -ce, -ci and z. **The lisp** is called **el seseo**, and I don't do el seseo porque el seseo es solo para los españoles. I learned to speak Spanish in Perú, so it's not for me. Pero me gusta el seseo en la palabra ejercicio. Try it! /E-hair-thi-thi-o/. Nothing could sound more *Julio Geordio*.

El ejercicio que me gusta incluye:

— Jumping to conclusiones;

— Pushing my luck; and

— Dodging deadlines.

También means **also**. Tambien me gusta doing diddly squats.

Use the Spanish

Give your opinion

- Me gusta el ejercicio = I like exercise
- No me gusta el ejercicio = I don't like exercise

LLAMA LLAMA

Do you know what a llama is? Es un animal domesticada de Suramérica, and people use them for their wool. If you have begun clases de español, they often start with what are you called. **¿Cómo te llamas? What are you called?** (Me llamo Ruth). Then they might go on to talk about your madre, and ask **what is she called: ¿cómo se llama?** They might continuar to talk about your pets, and ask what type of pet you have, and what is he called: ¿cómo se llama tu llama? (Se llama Alice).

— Una llama religiosa se llama the Dalai Llama.

La palabra for **very** is **muy**. If someone is **very fast**, they are **muuuuuuuuuuuuy rápido**.

— ¿Cómo se llama una llama muy rápida?
— Una Llamagini.

A film, or **movie**, is **una película. Una pelí** for short. If you say película, just make sure you don't say it peculiar. La pronunciación es /pe-li-coo-la/. There is no /yoo/ sound in película. You might prefer **books**, which are **libros**. You can find libros in the library. You might like libros y películas.

— ¿Cuál es la película favorita de mi llama?

— Llamadeus.

A man is **un hombre.** You can say **hombre**, like **man**! You can go to mirar un película en **un cine**, and that is the word for **cinema**, or **movie theatre.** Cine is pronounced /si-nay/. **Me gusta** is **I like**, and **I liked** is **me gustó.**

— Un hombre en el cine noticed mi llama sitting next to him.

— ¿Eres una llama? – el hombre asked, surprised.

— Sí.

— What are you doing en el cine?

— Mi llama respondió, - bueno, me gustó el libro.

Se llama Bob means **he is called Bob. Llama** also means **call**, like what you do to someone con un teléfono. **Llamame** means **call me**, as in **telephone me. Una llama** is also **a flame**, so **en llamas** means **in flames.** If you want to say, a llama in flames calls a llama in flames … you might want to say that, it might happen! In Spanish it would sound like this:

— Una llama en llamas llama a una llama en llamas.

* * * * *

TOILET HUMOR

A bit of vocabulario that could, potentially, be very useful is **toilet paper**. En español se llama **papel higiénico**, and you say papel /ee-hee-EN-ico/. You can practicar saying papel /ee-hee-EN-ico/. Or, you can say **/pay achay/**, which is how to say **P.H.** My cousin is mi prima, y el marido de mi prima se llama Stephen. That's Stephen con /pay achay/.

The street, or the road is **la calle**. Remember, double LL makes a /y/ sound, so say /cayay/.

— El papel higiénico no puede cruzar la calle.

— ¿Por qué?

— Porque it would get stuck in the crack.

94

España is made up of different regions, and the area that has Barcelona as its capital se llama Cataluña, Catalonia en inglés. En Cataluña there is una tradición navideña muy extraña. Se llama el caganer and it is literally a figurine of a shepherd at the nativity scene, with his trousers down, having a poo, while Mary cradles el bebé Jesús, con los ángeles, **los tres magos ... the three wise men** and all the normal people and animals you expect at the nativity scene. With el Caganer in the corner. El antropólogo catalán, Miguel Delgado, dice que la crucifixión de Jesucristo, una tortura y ejecución pública como símbolo de una religión, es mucho más grotesco que el caganer en la natividad. That is true, pero no es chistoso.

El Caganer basicamente translates as **the shitter**. En inglés we might say, - I nearly wet myself laughing. En español **laughter** is **la risa**, and **almost** is **casi**; y el equivalente de "**I almost wet myself laughing**" en español es: **casi me cago de risa**.

Navidad means **Christmas**, y en navidad we give and receive **presents**, which are called **regalos** en español.

— La navidad del año pasado, yo recibí papel higiénico sudoku.

— No es muy difícil. You can only fill it with number ones and number twos.

The toilet is normally called **el baño**. If you are **looking for** someone, you are **buscando** a that person. I wonder who or what buskers are looking for.

— Eeyore visitó el baño. ¿Por qué?

— Porque estaba buscando a Pooh.

Do you remember how to say **toilet paper**? **Papel higiénico**, or /pay achay/, P.H. **It rolled** is **rodó**, not too dissimilar. Rodó. **Down** is **abajo**, and **downhill** is **cuesta abajo**. **It rolled downhill** is, **rodó cuesta abajo**.

— ¿Por qué el papel higiénico rodó cuesta abajo?

— To reach the bottom.

Use the Spanish

When you need to go …

- El baño = The bathroom
- Papel higiénico = Toilet paper

COWS

Cows are **vacas** en español. Remember, the V has a /b/ sound. /Bacas/. Me gustan las vacas.

— Uno de los problemas de las vacas invisibles, is that they are herd but they are not seen.

The word for **lazy** is **perezozas**. La pronunciación es /pe-re-so-sas/, which is a lot of syllables for a lazy word.

— Cuáles son las vacas más perezosas?
— ¡Vacaciones!

Cuesta abajo means **downhill**, so what do you think cuesta arriba means? **Va** means **it goes**, **he goes** or **she goes**, so **una vaca va** means **a cow goes**. **Cuesta arriba** means **uphill**, by the way. Is that what you thought?

Si means **if**, and **sí** means **yes**. **Si estás**, means **if you are**, and **si ves**, means **if you see**.

— Si estás en una montaña, y si ves una vaca que va cuesta arriba, that is la crema, rising to the top.
— I think I have heard estos chistes de vacas before ... I have a real feeling of deja-moo.

A farmer is **un granjero**. **A farm** is **una granja**. George Orwell's novel, *Animal Farm*, está titulado *Rebelión en la granja* en español.

— Las vacas del granjero Brown son las más divertidas, often referred to as the laughing stock.

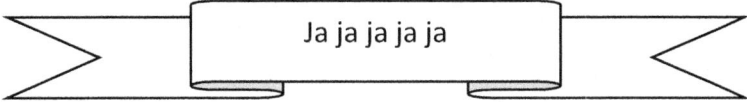

Ja ja ja ja ja

The word for **good** is **bueno**, and the word for **best** is **mejor**, pronounced /me-hor/. **A field** is **un campo**, which is easy to remember because you camp en un campo.

— La mejor vaca was outstanding en su campo.

Una vaca is **a cow**. **Una oveja** is **a sheep**. Si una vaca gets una vacación, does una oveja geta a standing ovation?

Me gusta la palabra nunca. **Nunca** means **never**, and I like the way it sounds. I used to live near a convent, and the nuns were terrifying drivers. You never wanted to be anywhere near the nuns' car. Nunca. **Cruces** means **you**

cross. Nunca cruces la calle in front of the nuns' car. If you did that, you would only do it once.[4]

— Nunca cruces una oveja furiosa con una vaca furiosa, or you will get unos animales in a very baaaad moooood.

Use the Spanish

A rural holiday?

- Vacas y ovejas = Cows and sheep
- El granjero = The farmer
- Los campos = The fields
- La granja = The farm

---

* * * * *

LOS DÍAS DE LA SEMANA

The days of the week are **los días de la semana** en español. Monday through to Friday is lunes, martes, miércoles, jueves y viernes. Lunes a viernes are named after heavenly bodies: the Moon, Mars, Mercury, Jupiter and Venus. The

---

[4] I'm sure not all nuns are the same, and there are probablemente some nuns who are very good and safe drivers.

names for the planets in Spanish are similar to los días de la semana that were named after them. La luna, Marte, Mercurio, Júpiter y Venus. Again, los días are lunes, martes, miércoles, jueves y viernes. When you have a test on los días de la semana en la escuela, you often find that el profesor shows his marvellous sentido de humor, by not giving you any marks because you wrote los días with capital letters.

You know that people say **today, hoy**, is a gift. **A gift** is **un regalo**. **A receipt** is **un recibo**, and to ask for a receipt say quiero un recibo. Remember, qu make a /k/ sound. With a receipt you can can a refund or you can **exchange it**, **cambiarlo**. Quiero cambiarlo. The word for **every** is **cada**.

— Cada día es un regalo.
— Yo quiero un recibo por el lunes. Quiero cambiarlo por otro viernes.

You can practice los días by asking yourself, **what comes after lunes**, what comes after jueves, and so on. En español, that is **¿qué va después de lunes? Después** means **after**. It sounds like /des-pwes/. It is a funny sound, like something a looney toons character like Daffy Duck or Bugs

Bunny might say: /des-pwes/. El próximo chiste is set **en una escuela, in a school**.

— José, ¿Qué planeta va después de Marte?
— Miércole.

Mañana is **tomorrow**, and that is a day too. Mañana is the word used to signal procrastination. Don't know what procrastination means? Look it up mañana.

Ayer means **yesterday**. Can you remember the word for yesterday? Ayer. Oh yeah!

Mi día favorito es hoy. **Hoy** means **today**, and because the letter H is mute, it sounds like OY. You can really put a bit of power into the word hoy.

The weather forecast often talks about hoy y mañana. **Cero grados = zero degrees**.

— Si hoy la temperatura es cero grados, y mañana va a ser twice as cold, how cold is it going to be mañana?

Nada means **nothing**. **Hace** means **does** or **is doing**.

— ¿Qué hace tu pez?
— Nada.

I started out with nada, and I still have most of it. Tengo todo el dinero que necesito – if I die by 4.00pm, hoy.

Entiendo is **I understand**, and **un entendimiento** is **an understanding**. I love the way that sounds: /en-tendy-mᵞento/. Nice, isn't it! You can get un entendimiento de palabras como arruina, by thinking about what it looks like. A good guess would be ruin, porque **arruina** contains the word **ruin**.

— Nada arruina un viernes más que un entendimiento de que hoy es martes.

I want to finish here with a quote, rather than a joke, from Dale Carnegie. The word for **remember** is **recuerda**. **You worried** is **preocupabas**. It is a difficult word to say, so start with -abas, .-pabas, -cupabas, -ocupabas, preocupabas. Easy, right?!

— Recuerda, hoy es el mañana del que te preocupabas ayer.

Hoy entiendes más español que ayer. When you practice something, you get better at it.

ADIÓS

The word for **chair** or **seat** is **silla**. The double LL makes a /y/ sound, so silla sounds like see ya! Imagina that you are in a full room. You are sitting on the floor because todas las sillas son ocupadas. Then someone gets up to go to the toilet. As you take their silla, you can say, see ya!

The word for **city** is **ciudad**. City and citizen and ciudad all come from the same Latin root. Ciudad sounds like this: /see-oo-dad/. Say bye to dad, he's going to the city. Ciudad.

My husband is **mi marido**. **My fridge** is **mi refrigerador**, similar to refrigerator. La pronunciación es /refree-hera-dor/. The word for **weird** or **strange** is **extraño**.

— Mi marido left una nota en el refrigerador, saying, esto no funciona.

— I opened el refrigerador y funciona bien. Extraño.

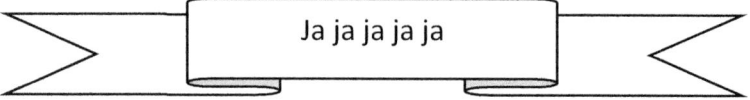

Ja ja ja ja ja

A kiss is **un beso**. En inglés we can write a kiss with the letter x. En español, an x does not mean a kiss, and yet the way the letter **x** sounds en español is /**a-kees**/. Extraño. So if you want to put **kisses** on una nota in Spanish, you have to write "**besos**."

Mi marido is **my husband**, and **mi vecino** is **my neighbour**. The V sounds like a /b/, so say /besino/. It sounds like a Spanish word for a little kiss, un besino. Give me un beso, give me un besino. A female neighbour is una vecina.

When I lived in Perú there was **an advert**, **una publicidad**, that I liked. It was for parecetamol, and the escenario era un niño had hit his head on the cupboard door. La madre hit the door, and said, "**malo, malo, malo (bad, bad, bad)**. **¡Tú no haces eso!**" That means, **you don't do that**! ¡Tú no haces eso! So to say, **why don't you do that**, say, **¿por qúe tú no haces eso?**

— Mi marido said to me, our new vecina always gives un beso a su marido when she goes off to el trabajo. ¿Por qué tú no haces eso?
— ¿Cómo puedo? I don't even know him.

You know that **goodbye** is **adiós**, but **to say goodbye** is **despedirse**. Es completamente diferente. When I left Perú, I had a **goodbye party**, and that was called mi **despedida**, my **farewell party**. **He said goodbye**, is **se despidió**.

— ¿Cómo se despidió el MP3 del CD?
— Audios.

I hope you have learned un poco de español reading this book, and I hope you have been entertained. All good things come to an end, y es hora de despedirnos and say adiós. Just before you go though, here are a couple of ways to say, see you later aligator.

Un pato is **a duck**, and **un patito** is **a duckling**. **Un rato** is **a while**, not to be confused with **una rata**, which is a **rat**. **See you** is **nos vemos**; it literally means **we will see us**. **Nos vemos**.

— Nos vemos al ratito, patito.

Una alimaña is **a pest**. Say /ali-man-ya/. **A rat** is **una rata**, y las ratas son alimañas. **Una alimaña** is also the word for a **despicable person**, so I hope you know I'm joking when I say:

— Hasta mañana, alimaña.

Adiós.

* * * * *

MIS RECOMENDACIONES

Sentido de humor is **sense of humor**. If you like mi sentido de humor, you will love Mafalda. Recomiendo this lovely cartoon, by the Argentinian autór, Quino. Reading what young Mafalda has to say, with the drawings to help you understand, will be a great help to your progress with the Spanish lenguaje. You can always use Google translate to help you. Download the app, and if you use the camera function you can point your camera at Spanish text and it will give you a translation. Sure, the translations are not always perfecto, but it is still a great way to continuar con tu español. Y es divertido.

Another thing you can do to practicar tu español is listen to songs. It is easy to get the words, and the translations, and learn to lip-sync. You can even video your performance. If you have rehearsed, it will look great. Of course, if you liked this book you might have a taste for funny stuff, so here are three songs I think are quite funny to get you started.

Mayonesa is a song about a guy who gets to dance with a woman he finds attractive in a nightclub. The problem is he has drunk too much and she shakes him up like she was making mayonaise and all the drink goes to his head, so he doesn't know where he lives or what he's called. And he doesn't care.

La guitarra, by Los Auténticos Decadentes, is a song about a young man who still lives with his family. His problem is the opinion of his family who would like him to earn his living. His revelation is that his life is the guitar, home-cooking, his dad's beer and the bank of dad. He knows what he wants … to play the guitar and have people fall in love with his voice. This is at odds with what his family want, regarding getting up, getting shaved and getting out.

The last song I am going to mencionar is by a band called Azul Azul, and the song is called **Mamá no quiero comer más huevo, mum I don't want to eat any more eggs**. It is about a guy whose mum makes him an egg, and if that doesn't fill him up she makes him two. For breakfast he has ham and egg, rice and egg for lunch, and egg salad for dinner, and now he doesn't like eggs. Everyone is getting fat eating eggs, and he is having **nightmares, pesadillas** about eating **omelettes, tortillas**. The chorus is ¡**Qué huevada**! In the part of Latin America this song comes from, **una huevada** is **a nest of eggs**, but it also means **a**

stupid thing, a crazy idea, or **a load of nonsense**. You should also be aware that throughout the Spanish world it is common to refer to **testicles** as **huevos**, the Spanish word for eggs.

By the time you are lip-syncing a few funny songs, you will feel confident and proud of your español.

My final tip for learning español, is to take some of your favourite quotes and chistes españoles, and turn them into posters or works of art to put up on your walls. If you do any you are happy with, don't forget to share them with me on my Facebook page, Spanglish Fantastico. I look forward to hearing from you. Hasta la vista, baby!

Spanglish Fantastico publishes a range of resources enabling you to improve your Spanish.

- Ruth Darby's Short Spanish Lessons freely available on Youtube
- Spanglish Fantastico is a full length Spanglish instructional reader, available on Amazon
- Family Spanish is a more advanced Spanglish reader for parents, with ideas and activities to help promote Spanish in the family setting.

SPANGLISH FANTÁSTICO

Contact through Spanglish Fantastico page on Facebook

Printed in Great Britain
by Amazon

87614856R00068